ragged edges

poems from the margins

ragged edges

poems from the margins

charles r. ringma

R
Regent College Publishing
www.regentpublishing.com

for

those who can still

dream and long and hope and dance

Published 2008 by Regent College Publishing
5800 University Boulevard, Vancouver, BC V6T 2E4 Canada
Web: www.regentpublishing.com
E-mail: info@regentpublishing.com

Regent College Publishing is an imprint of the Regent College Bookstore
<www.regentbookstore.com>. Views expressed in works published by Regent
College Publishing are those of the author and do not necessarily represent the
official position of Regent College <www.regent-college.edu>.

Book design by Robert Hand
<roberthandcommunications.com>

ISBN-10: 1-57383-420-3
ISBN-13: 978-1-57383-420-9

Library and Archives Canada Cataloguing in Publication

Ringma, Charles
Ragged edges: poems from the margins / Charles Ringma.

ISBN 978-1-57383-420-9

I. Title.

PS8635.I54R33 2008   C811'.6   C2008-900249-0

contents

preface / *xi*

a troubled seeker / 13

the weight of mystery / 15

the colonialists / 17

a soft touch / 19

the woman / 21

the silent searcher / 23

the man / 25

the tear / 27

the sentinels / 29

penetration of the dove / 31

the monks / 33

the alarm clock / 37

life's dialectic / 39

the shattered glass / 41

enough / 45

the red fire-extinguisher / 47

unreconciled / 51

at norrie's beach / 53

the boy / 55

a different death / 57

central queensland twilight / 59

hope / 61

mocking the mystery / 63

at prayer / 65

words / 69

waiting / 71

growth / 73

haunted / 75

the couple / 77

suicide / 79

sons of the reformation / 83

fragile love / 87

humility / 89

the ocean / 91

the hospital ward / 93

pregnancy / 97

empty words / 99

those eyes / 101

soaring upward / 105

suspended / 107

forsaken / 109

labour ready (i) / 111

labour ready (ii) / 115

the faithful / 117

intimacy / 121

being found / 123

pre- and post-creation / 125

manila / 127

two hands / 133

the moon / 135

dreams / 137

embedded / 139

o'reilly's / 141

power / 143

love / 145

skin / 147

questions / 151

the kiss / 155

east vancouver night / 157

this young man geoffrey / 161

your own life? / 167

broken community / 169

ode to a loved one / 173

into the great silence / 177

a night in greenwich village / 179

seeking journey / 183

the dreamer / 185

reflection / 187

the womb of god / 191

time / 193

preface

Life can be talked about. It can also be analysed. But
first and foremost it needs to be lived. A story can be
understood in terms of structure. But first it must be told.

And what of poetry? It should need no introduction. It is
an invitation to read.

So I will say nothing about the circumstances under
which these poems were written other than that they span
over a long period of time and that they came from spaces
of difficulty rather than the landscapes of tranquility.

There is nothing neat and tidy about life. It is both full of
hope and very messy. There are always ragged edges. But
edges suggest that there is terrain one has traversed.

Charles Ringma
Brisbane, Australia
2007

a troubled seeker

there is nothing winsome
about you, o, difficult one.

you are playful in your wildness
severe in your mercy
tempestuous in your silence
bounded in your power

silent in your speaking
and frightening in your spirit.

and yet i draw closer
with tiptoe curiosity
sculpted out of an ancient memory

of having known you
when you danced
before the world
became your brutal burden.

the weight of mystery

o, dark and mysterious one.
the promised presence
who hides in silence
of the darkest cave
and in whispers
of the fading wind.

how much we want
to pull you out of
your hiding places
so that we may hear
the words that scatter our fears
and heal our woundedness.

but having heard
we are afraid
and long for the
silence of the early dawn
the mellow embrace of winter's dark
the forgotten grave
the musings of the heart.

we cannot bear
your silence
or your speaking.
both are a crippling load.
we cannot hold your heaviness
in our fragile hands.

the colonialists

little wonder that they
sought the far horizons
looking for a world
beyond the bigotries
that sprayed the fields
with royal and religious blood.

find a new world, they did.
pregnant with innocence
and carnal with exotic possibilities.

but their own wounded world
held them in its cloning clasp
blinding the eyes
twisting grasping fingers.

and so they recreated their own image
in the other's virgin innocence
that in plunder and rape
was never meant
to father such a sickly child.

a soft touch

touching.
ever so lightly
touching.
like a whisper of silk.
the caress of the gentlest breeze.

touching.
fingers gently
touching.
not holding.
not withdrawing.
not straying.
simply like children playing.

touching.
fingers ever so lightly
touching.
divining a rhythmic dance
to sacred tune.
that ends too soon.

touching.
ever so gently
touching.
not asserting.
not averting.
just playing.
but saying
deep matters of the heart.

the woman

lithe and rhythmic as the brolga dance
controlled and subtle as a feline's advance
a sensual form draped in meekness
a quivering deer in poised sleekness
hurt winged duck among the rushes
hidden tears and quiet blushes
with clear clarion call on crisp night air
with anguished bowing in restless prayer
the rush of time and hectic pace
etched lines on strong yet caring face
a mystery clothed in womanhood
unique and seldom understood
yet pushes on with burdened haste
to find her unambiguous place
but even then will never rest
until she is the bridegroom's guest

the silent searcher

i looked for your imprints
in the ancient forests
home of millenia of storm clouds,
antarctic beech and the tousle of vines.

i looked for the marks of your fingers
in the starry heavens
theatre of a million lights
all pointing in no direction.

i looked for your heart
in the depths of my scarred being
but found only the echoes of silence
and the pain of emptiness.

and so i looked no more
but waited with longing to be found
by the illusive lover
whose absence finds us everywhere.

the man

with unsteady step
he makes his weary way forward.
    all alone.
a sombre silence pervades him
wrapping him in shrouded solitude.
    all embracing.
the shoulders weighted and stooped
carry an unbearable world.
    all inward.
no observer's curious eye however
can unveil this man's woundedness.
    all hidden.
the furrowed lines of grief
lie evident in the relentless march of time.
    all unrecoverable.
he is not going anywhere
and comes from what should never be remembered.
    all's lost.
he stumbles and falls
a wounded deer never to rise.
    all has ended.
except a wrenching cry escapes him
it echoes through all the wars and follies of our time.

the tear

all the words had fallen in disarray.
only an empty silence remained.

it fell.
a solitary glistening tear
from a sorrowful heart
that had wept itself empty.

catching the sun's effusive light
it sparkled for but a moment.
a blotch was all that remained
and an aching heart.

the sentinels

they stand there
    still
like sentinels.
the green-leafed duty-men.
in scattered rows
all in their place.
    stiff
yet with their gentle swaying
almost as if they are saying
can you await
your simple fate
until the aged roots give way
and crashing to the ground
    decay.
to make a way
for sapling green.

penetration of the dove

sperming creation
filling the void
shaping tangled masses
holding sea from soil.

colouring the darkness
stronging the weak
falling on prophets
impelling to speak.

is the genesis.

pregnating a maiden
deafening a priest
inspiring the baptist
preparing god's feast.
blinding the blind eyes
gathering the meek
debacling the proudest.

is the first day of the week.

the monks

like the rest of us
these men were torn
whimpering from their mother's womb.

  a bloody mess!

and shaped by fragile families
they began their uncertain journeys
into a fractured and wounded world.

  what folly and risk!

strengthening yet hiding their vulnerable egos
they added to their lives
education, achievements, lovers, conquests.

  the making of the social self!

but they did not find their true home
they were refugees in familiar places
pilgrims in the bosom of the church
strangers in the midst of their own successes.

  the sound of a different drummer!

they became enchanted
by the whispers of the ancient spirit
murmuring brotherhood, unity, love
the koinonia of the followers of jeshua.

that beguiling vision!

and so they turned
to the womb of the trinity
birthing community
life together through the sustaining spirit.

such goodness in such fragile hands!

they now live as midwives
for all who still wander
bearing their pain
in the bowing of prayer and the gift of hospitality.

the birthpangs of a new world!

the alarm clock

be.
being.
being with.
talking.
knowing.
touching.
joining.
falling...
spiralling downwards
into nothingness filled with the lightness of being.
drifting... ever drifting...
awakening.
the whispers of a familiar world.
the alarm clock rings with a note of finality.
another day at the office.

life's dialectic

in the birthing is the aging.
in the living a slow diminishing.
in the growing so seldom knowing.
in the gaining always losing.
in the choices hardly choosing.
in the goodbyes a little dying.

but in the leaving awaits a returning.
in the releasing a finding.
in the grieving lies a relieving.
in the denying a blessed receiving.
in the emptiness a holding.
in the mystery an unfolding.

the shattered glass

drawn from the red earth
scarred by human hand
nurtured on twisted vines
blasted by the fiercest of suns
(one would have thought that nothing
could grow there
except the dust of broken dreams).

yet each year the green shoots appeared
on gnarled wood all but dead.
and in time the muscat grapes hung
lush like pubescent breasts
throbbing with the nectar of life.

picked, squeezed, processed and bottled
the fruit of the vine
lies in sullen forgetfulness
in regimented rows
in the bowels of the dark.
a bloodlike fluid
in aging transformation
pulsating with a power
to gladden the human heart.

and on that festive occasion
exploding from its long captivity
ruby red in the noonday sun
it cascaded into a sparkling glass
swirling, it shattered it.
descending, dripping
it oozed away
denying consumptive pleasure
scorning the hand that held it
it returned to its very beginning
leaving the stain of golgotha's red.

enough

i have no need to see you—
    the eye of the storm
    the flight of the eagle
    the blush of the maiden
    the broken bread
these are enough.

golgotha was far too brutal.
an affront to goodness and humanity.
and the wounds of the world
lie open there like rotting sores.

one cannot gaze for long at such a sight.
one is repulsed by one's own complicity
and the horror of god's way of love.

so just whisper in the night breeze.
and skim the seas with the froth of your voice.
reveal yourself in the cry of the newborn;
in the murmurings of lovers;
the mellow hues of the setting sun.
and in your broken mended ones
as they bow in anxious prayer.

this is enough.
i cannot hear in any other way.
yet golgotha still echoes across the ages
and calls me to embrace its confronting voice.

the red fire-extinguisher

the small grotto
built into the wall
once contained
the madonna,
or a statue of the sympathetic christ,
or a guardian saint, perhaps.

they would watch the quickened pace of doctors
the gentle movement of nurses
the shuffles of patients with scars and drips.

their stony stares
were not indifferent
to the human traffic along the hospital corridor.
and for those who took the time
to see beyond their stylised imagery
to a world of faith, reverence and prayer,
these sign-posts to another world
have long gone.

nuns no longer bustle in this place of healing.
they are mere ghosts lacking embodiment and visibility.
and a fire-extinguisher now graces the grotto.
a functional necessity in an age where faith is foolishness.

the fire extinguisher is hardly necessary.
the fire has long gone out that drew women into
celibacy and community and selfless service.
those who shuffle along these corridors
have nowhere to gaze in faith.
the profaned grotto echoes a silent eternity.
there is no hope beyond the scalpel and the needle.

unreconciled

when the last prayer has been offered,
the whispered promise unheeded,
a gentle touch unacknowledged,
and the visit unreturned.

with the pain of parting duller,
our feelings numb but tender,
the dreaming all but perished in the wasteland of our hopes.

when the shame of unfulfilment
weakens future resolution,
and the dregs of bitterness
quell no thirst,
but fan the flames.
and no reconciliation is offered,
for no partner is envisaged—
then our dreaming embalmed in winter,
becomes the springtime of our tears.

at norrie's beach

and the old man
with bright red ball
and pursuing dog
oblivious to all
in his innocent game
recaptures a frame
of childhood freedom.

the boy

he sits there squat.
a little crumpled ball.
staring wild-eyed in the mirror.
as scissors click
and mum reproves
his wriggling in the chair.

the ordeal is done.
the barber smiles.
a jellybean is offered.
he looks once more
and wonders why
he's now so very different.

a different death

we are at best
one breath away
from a whimpering demise.

pristine beauty
physical strength
laudable achievements
cover our fragility
with paper-thin veneer.

if only we had become contemplatives
of the empty grave
rather than filling it with our diversions
we may have lived differently.
such a life we owed
not only to ourselves
but also to others
whom we goaded and oppressed
through the fractures of our own being.

physical death may bring
a tormented peace.
a contemplative death
seeds of release.

central queensland twilight

a sacred silence
blankets a sun-blanched land
caressing an unyielding day
in the approaching twilight hour.

the harsh contours become muted
long shadows finger yellow grasses
stark ridges tinge to golden hue
as the queen of heaven descends her fiery throne.

a sigh of silence embalms the fading view
broken by the noisy miner's shrilly cry
and soft murmurings from a pale-headed rosella
make a benediction of day's end.

enshrouded the earth retreats
with hastening step
into the abyss of darkness
entombed in restless slumber
to await a new enthronement.

hope

is there much hope
fair child of mine
in a world so grossly marred
by hate, avarice and genocide?

i would say not
but willingly lie
to still the question
and erase the frown
that's on your brow.

but my protection
cannot keep
the haunting ghosts
that taunt your sleep
and disappointments
that go deep.

you're on your own
but not alone
and hope comes from the future
and in your quest to do your best
be not afraid
for what you are you cannot lose
though everything is taken.

and faith in god
though sorely tried
is never fully shaken.

mocking the mystery

unknowingness
unmeasurability
is the mystery of your person.

which in foolishness
and grasping haste
i seek to unmantle.

in this fatal doing
i find the mystery gone.

at prayer

the remaining solitary silent are at prayer.
the ritual noises of the sanctuary have ceased.
most of the early morning faithful have spilled into the street.
but their songs linger like caressing echoes.
and the words of good news rest in the wooden rafters.

the altar lies bundled in a shroud waiting a new unveiling.
the priest has rushed into the other duties of his day.
only the twittering birds break the brooding silence
while the remaining faithful gaze in reflection and adoration
silent like the statues to which their faces are beholden.

worshipper and image somehow merge.
the human and divine co-mingle.
mortals penetrating the unpenetrable.
faith merges with sight.

the sudden patter of shoeless feet
slap the cold marble stones like an unholy intrusion.
a child's grubby hands are thrust in the faces of the adoring
    faithful.
the holy christ seems to vanish from view.
the words of the beggar child are insistent.
the religious spell is broken; prayer has ended.

the solitary silent fall into words of disapproval.
the beggar child is waved away, empty-handed.
the embodied voice of poverty has entered the sacred place.
the grubby mundane has disrupted a holy piety.
an uneasy conscience remains.
faith without heart and hands.

but the presence has gone.
it may have disappeared with the waif-like child.

words

like a busy weaver's shuttle
my words to you...
fly.

measured, tempered
yet revealing
and asking...
why.

but forming no pattern
mosaic or rhyme
they falter and waver
and end in a...
sigh.

left unattended
and with no reply
they spiral downwards and...
die.

waiting

we are the faded
imprints
of your creativity
worn in the sands
of time.

hidden and colourless
and under
no one's thoughtful gaze
except your own
we wait for the winds of god
to reconfigure us.

growth

the single way
unheeded, with methodical step—
one, two, three…
is the wishdream.

the other road
impeded, with faltering step—
one, two, three…
is reality.

dual roads
conflicting with anguish and decision—
this way, that way, which
is the royal way to painful growth.

haunted

limp leaves in unswaying trees
await the blast of summer sun.
the first inklings of its coming
have barely smudged night's fading black.
the call of the frogmouthed owl is already silent
waiting for the kookaburra's herald of a new dawn.

nature and the city's streets lie jointly still
yet i lie troubled with conflicting thoughts
unable to be herded into sense or explanation.
like vague shadows haunting my horizon
defying clarity and hopefulness
they march relentlessly
these phantoms mocking in victory.

is it failure or despair?
is it a fracturing of a tinsel inner cohesion?
is it a troubled conscience?
is it a mocking demon?
is it my shadow with its unwelcome call?

i know not.
wisdom has forsaken me.
insight has strayed.
i am so afraid.
but into your hands, o god, i commit my troubled spirit.

the couple

i saw them walking
ever so slowly
with wrinkled feet
in ill-fitting shoes.

the flotsam of a society
that knows only
productivity and success
the shoes tell the sorry tale.

they leaned together against the blustering wind.
not a word passed between them.
they sheltered in each other's presence
woven in a tapestry of suffering togetherness.

suicide

she lies there still.
a crumpled form.
assailed by no one
other than her own despair.

no one's victim?
but stifled by conjugal love.
the matrimonial holocaust
has done its dreaded deed!

there is no law of just returns.
there are only victims.
with love spent and resources gone
the spirit uprooted
from all that is normal and reciprocal
ebbs away into an eternal sigh.

in spasms it seeks to grasp.
it claws for a foothold.
but it can only whimper.
and sigh the sigh of death.

for if the present holds no offer of life
what can a dark future bring?
if one's loved ones offer no hope
what is the gift of a stranger?
if life has no meaning
what can the white-clad helper do?

crushed in the clasp of despair
the final energies are summoned
to embrace an awful death.

a crumpled form.
a throw-away ragged doll.
from this some life may yet flow.
but only for others.

the sons of the reformation

the lands that gave us
luther, calvin, knox
also fathered other sons
nietzsche, sartre, marx
the highpriests of despair, "freedom" and oppression.
their incantations still scar the heart of europe
but bring it no relief
and no worship
only a muted sigh
or the militant cry
or the irrational hope
or the wish to die.

but the sons of reformation
squandered their voice.
they masked their lord.
divided his word.
took up the sword.
embraced the state.
and sealed their fate.

can the womb of europe
bring forth other offspring?
women of peace.
men of reconciliation.
workers for justice.
people of the gospel

who bring hope, spirit and life
in the midst of strife?

may the god who spoke and it was done
have the last word in his son.
and in all who follow him
whether they die or win.

fragile love

sometimes, i would love daringly.
each broken friendship to reclaim
every debtor to repay
all need to face
with your amazing grace.

sometimes, i would love wrongfully.
desiring what i cannot have
fantasizing person and place
building pregnant imagination
into tinsel imitation.

but mostly, i love intermittently.
greater moments subverted by commonality.
opportunities sacrificed to banality.
showing my humanity.
while reaching for eternity.

humility

if i cannot say,
"i do not know"
and "much has failed"
i'll never find
my deepest self
or someone's helping hand.
my cry for help
will never come
with weakness unexposed
and i will die an inner death
destroying healthful growth.

the ocean

these white-flecked rows
in rhythmic beat
crash upon the shore
momentarily awash.
and grope their way
to penetrable dunes
till nature bids them, turn.

the hospital ward

it's 2 a.m.
the long night
marches ever so slowly
to a never appearing grey dawn.

the sleep of forgetfulness
has long eluded me.
and neither sleeping pills or pain killers
have carried me away to its elusive shores.

i am not alone.
but keep harassed and reluctant company
with every fart
groan
bed bell
footstep
whisper
hum of air-conditioners
flushing of toilets
and the continued cry of the old woman
with her mutterings
warding off the spirits
that invite her to the gloomy nether-world.

the city streets have long fallen silent.
the lights of nearby homes are dimmed.
the hospital ward shrouded in muted darkness

pulsates with the pain of a broken humanity.
fevers of mind and body
traumas of accidents
survivors of invasive surgery
the groans of loss, fear and vulnerability.

i am a participant in this medical symphony
wishing that the musical odyssey would end.
but it drags on to a greying dawn
and the first tentative steps to recovery
that leaves one scarred forever.

pregnancy

o, empty virginal womb
opulent in its fruitfulness
but barren in its denial of forbidden love.

how you weep
the lament of the ages
of a death
that leaves no prodigy.

this long asceticism
may become the tomb
that engulfs love and creativity
into a sterile mediocrity.

it may also be the seedbed
where life for others
is the begetting
of the daughters of god.

empty words

the many words spoken in
love
reaction
question
and pain
hang on the horizon
like a tottering pier
battered by relentless waves
that have left it
like an old man's missing teeth.

fallen into disarray
and irretrievable in their disrepair
these words await
their sullen fate.

more words won't salvage the wreck.
only the whispers of the breeze
the silence of the deep
the waning of the moon
the tears of grief
the murmurs of the heart
the renewing spirit
can caress such searing pain.

those eyes

thinking eyes:
observing, absorbing, analysing, evaluating, clarifying...
and gently, ever so gently, yet firmly
speaking.

wistful eyes:
longing, brooding, hoping, wanting...
and gently, ever so gently, and passionately
dreaming.

hooded eyes:
withholding, guarding, masking, protecting...
and gently, ever so gently, and carefully
excluding.

mischievous eyes:
playing, teasing, joking, beckoning...
and gently, ever so gently, and carefully
welcoming.

loving eyes:
caring, trusting, sharing, joining...
and gently, ever so gently, and generously
giving.

discerning eyes:
praying, reflecting, perceiving, critiquing...

and gently, ever so gently, believing and
disbelieving.

or have my eyes failed to see
the inner eye of thee?

soaring upward

twelve palestinians
are present at the parting feast of bread and wine.
amidst their laughter, whispers, and song
hangs a question:
poised in the air like the cuckoo shrike
arrested in flight by the markman's arrow.

silently it hurtles down
wings suspended.
is this the flight of death?
or ploy
to thwart the markman's second chance?

is this the night where dreams are dashed?
the meal a grim farewell?
the grey shrike's flight of death?

the giant groves reach to receive
the stricken prey.
the marksman holds his breath.
but the cuckoo with upturned wings
soars beyond its death.

suspended

i come running
as someone who hesitatingly waits—
for the black hood's removal
before the iron
makes its gravitational plunge.
for the monarch's nod
that offers a pardon.
for the raised eyebrow
that augurs a lover's tryst.

suspended.
the heart soars and plunges
with wings of craving love.
the mind circles
with hopes and fears
but remains clasped in iron bands
stronger than the executioner's
rusty pike.

forsaken

even the faintest whisper
like searching fingers
touching delicate skin
would have been enough.

but silence greets me
the muted voice of the void.
the echo of the tomb.
with its paralysing fear.

i had hoped for presence and welcome
the caress of comfort and care.
but once again i descend the staircase
into the long loneliness
where no one is waiting
only my own grieving heart.

labour ready (i)

under the brutal colours
of the dusty noonday sun
they wait
these hulks of humanity
the day labourers
of the palestinian road
immortalised in gospel story
but forgotten in the praxis of the church.

in the 5 a.m. darkness
of the vancouver winter
they wait
at labour ready
these same day labourers
forgotten in the city of leisure
that knowingly exploits them.

two millennia lie between them.
but they are linked by a snaking cord of injustice.
they are bound together
as if the same mother had agonisingly spewed them
from a watery cocoon
into a harsh social darkness
that neither nurtures or protects.

so they wait
only to return

to face the scornful eyes
of tired lovers
and the averted gaze
of children wrapped in a tapestry of shame.

not wanted by the captains of industry
and the maestros of progress
they are an embarrassment
to their own families
unknown to neighbours
and cursed by the womb
that brought them forth in such hope
and rapturous expectation.

these are the shadow-dwellers.
their broken lineage pockmarks the veins of history.
on the margins of society
they have but one carefully crafted skill.
they know what it is to wait.

labour ready (ii)

they are haunting and unwanted spectres
these day labourers
of the dusty noonday palestinian road.

frozen for posterity
in the brazen frame of gospel story
they snake their way through history as a long sigh.

in the early winter mornings
while vancouver lies enfolded in uncaring sleep
these same men linger at labour ready.

they wait for the call
to give their meagre strength and skill
or absorb the daily dismissal.

waiting blurs into a time suspension
they have no courage
to face their spouses' scornful stare.

the flotsam of our economies
know no gospel of grace
only the 5 a.m. wait of the next day.

the faithful

the early morning
hangs suspended by a smog-enshrouded sun.
its strange light filters into the sanctuary
through windows of colour and symbol
and embalms the solitary faithful at prayer.

silent and yet moving lips.
upturned glances.
trembling hands.
the rustle of turning pages of the ancient book.
the rhythmic fingering of holy beads.
the manila sun envelops them all.

but there are also deep shadows
on the faces of the faithful.
an old lady shuffles out into the noisy street.
deep lines scar her face.
it seems that all the wars have made her their battlegound.
stooped and unsteady she disappears.
holy beads dangling aimlessly in gnarled hands.

the light intensifies.
shadows deepen.
the faithful one by one
have moved into the busy street
the hum of traffic
the distant cry of children's voices.

the memory of the old lady lingers.
did she come seeking? what did she find?
was she burdened? did love lighten the load?
did the book bring a message?
the beads a sacramental hope?
the pock-marked lines on her face remain, was her spirit
renewed?

intimacy

as soft
as the caress of the gentlest breeze
fondling the upturned cheek;
softer
than rain-drenched moss
absorbing the careful footstep;
so soft
that the whisper is too loud
fallen snow too hard
shorn wool too irritating.

soft yet firm
twin peaks defying the open sky
thrusting bounded earth into the heavens.
the pinnacles of womanhood.
nurturing fountains
invitations to intimacy
homing place of the wayward wanderer
lost in a wilderness of his own making.

here welcome is passion
and passion spent is bliss
and bliss sacraments a joining
where two are truly one.

being found

is this the valley of uncertainty
with its sullen autumn mists
swirling and engulfing
man, land and beast?

or is this the mountain clarity
with its springtime hues
sparkling in the noontime sun
drawing the gaze to yonder horizons?

it matters not
where one stands or what the season.
in the valley one may find an unexpected lantern.
on the mountain the curse of blinding light.

where one looks gives not the gift of insight.
the outward gaze may lead to distraction.
the inner glance may expose our dividedness.
so how then do we see and find the way?

we do not find the way and cannot see.
eyes need to be opened and the way finds us
as we hold the hand and are gently led
by the man who suffered in our stead.

pre- and post-creation

before the void
and time and space
the earth and all the human race
god knew it all
and laughed.

and in our time and frenzied space
and all the folly of the race
god knows it all
and sighs.

so in our time
and wounded race
god came to take our place
and cried.

manila

there she lies.
manila.
the hoped-for paris of the orient
like a battered doll
smothered in religious shroud
woven from the vomit of its myriad of jeepneys.

like moving spectres from a primeval forest
its defiant buildings briefly stumble into sight
in the early morn's awakening
only to retreat again in nether gloom.

one wonders whether seeing eye
or feverish imagination
created this momentary visibility.

like a motley array of the presidential guard
the clouds hold rank
this blanket of brown of human making
bidding them stay.

the air is still in its midday slumber.
there is no cheek's caress.
the trees on this mountaintop overlooking the city
hang limped and dejected.
the birds are hushed in the heated breath of sun.

in the shimmering distance
down the mountain
the city moves and vibrates
and excretes its human voices, traffic and the hum of factories.
and enfolds all as in a woman's billowing skirt.

the great city
so full of promise
having welcomed its millions
lies overwhelmed in the blanket of modernity
crippled by the folly of impossible dreams.

a lurid sun
sinks towards the bay
for its daily baptism
hallowing the city in sacred light.
a late breeze has left the city naked and exposed
its tall buildings like phallic symbols
make their final exposure
before the quickening steps of hurried night.

it is an uneasy midnight.
the mountain top lies in slumber.
the city below is morphosed in a million dwindling lights.
it vibrates still.
it knows little rest
in its fevered pace for progress.

a husband lies exhausted in bed.
he coughs and stirs
fretful dreams beset him.
one arm is flung aimlessly over his wife's buttocks.
the woman sleeps peacefully
an infant suckling at her breast.
a whisp of street light
falls on the christ of the crucifix
ever watchful until another day
in this city of dreams.

two hands

two hands.
the one so crowdedly full.
the other so achingly empty.

two hands.
the one so strongly holding.
the other so tenuously letting go.

two hands.
the one the servant of commitment.
the other the midwife of a captivating dream.

two hands.
two conflicting dreams?
should they become one?
the empty hand collapsing in fullness?
fullness spilling over to fill the empty hand?

what about the one-handed solution?
creating disability.
resolution through the quivering knife.
the easy option.
eliminating ambiguity and pain.

i have the gift of two hands.
the one that holds
the other that withholds
is my path of joy and pain.

the moon

draped in drifting clouds
embellishing its aloofness
the sullen and silent moon
suddenly unveiled
offers no word of comfort.

though it is often thought
that it whispers to lovers
incites the deranged
sculpts the cultic
makes archetypal connections,
i experience none of this
from that glacial white ball
suspended above the distant horizon.

i worriedly ponder:
am i not seeing or hearing?
so devoid of mystery?
so lacking imagination?
so locked in brutal rationality?

i do need to hear the moon's whispers.
i can tell.
to break the spell
and set the pace
from outer space
to reach this cold heart of mine.

dreams

dreams
these winged birds of the future
fly.

defying gravity
they soar beyond the clouds
drifting on pockets of upper air.
moving
gliding
resting.

the marks of the rhythm of transcendence.
signs of the birth of becoming.
membranes of the trauma of hope.

but dreams not only propel us forward
to what is yet to be
to a hoped-for horizon.
they may also pull us backward.
to the scarred places of fear
to woundedness that mars us all
to an immanence
that textures our humanity.

embedded

like rows of scattered oysters
impregnated on a craggy reef
we are embedded in this world
subject to wind and tide.

sustained by being chained
we seek to rise from our long prison
grasping an empty freedom
that cuts us off
from the nourishing sources of life.

we don't want to be held
in time or place.
we want to fly.
but oysters above the tide line
are easy pickings.

o'reilly's

home of millennia of storm clouds
and the darkest of forest.
how you languish
under barren skies
and the most brutal of suns.

like shrivelled breasts of an old woman
without even a hint of sustenance
giant staghorns like stricken birds
lie scattered on dusty paths
weeping a lament of the ages.

but the brazen skies
weep not
their sullen stare
reflects only the sun's
blistering contempt.

power

we might like to be
but we are not gods.
the primordial dust
not only clings closely
but shapes the very fabric of our being
even though we are marked by spirit.

but our longings
form our desires
and propel us to grasp
what fragile hands were never meant to hold.

we should be held, but want to hold.
holding we seek to possess.
possessing we seek to control.
controlling we crush
and in this madness
we think we have drunk the nectar of omnipotence.

but we are poisoned
by power's fatal chalice.
and become dust
devoid of human spirit.

love

is love
the winged arrow
that ever so surely flies
from cupid's mischievous bow
to find its quivering mark
in unsuspecting heart?

or is love
the nectar of the gods
the fruit of human mystery
tricklings out of caverns deep
that feed tempestuous streams
making love more than what it seems?

skin

skin.
the delicate clothing of our humanity
the sensitive covering of the pulsating machinations
of the body
a skein of beauty sheltering muscle, artery and bone.

skin.
the careful covering of the inner person
and the awesome revealing of the self
in the freedom of a shameless nakedness
under the gaze of the beloved.

skin.
the luring invitation to the wonder of touch
the softness of rustling satin
the coolness of an underground spring
the warmth of summer's embalming sun.

skin.
to touch its hunger
feeds the passions of the heart
makes the soul melodious
joins humanity and eternity.

skin.
the fabric of the membranes
of one's innermost being.

the outward touch to the innermost heart.
the veil never rent yet fully transluscent.
the harpstrings of the soul.

may i touch you, fully?

questions

   questions:
like electric barbs
quivering sensitive flesh;
like icy fingers
shocking a warm heart.
   searing.
   numbing.

   questions:
like shafts of morning light
exposing the dust and rubble of a ruined hacienda;
like the meanderings of an ancient brook
shaping the gorge that channels it.
   enlightening.
   forming.

   questions:
like an open hatch for a caged bird
offering an alluring freedom;
like a mysterious allusion
opening possibilities and hope.
   freeing.
   renewing.

    questions:
reluctant steps of pain.
uncertain strides of hope.
exploding the sameness of our bitter existence.
inviting us into the wide places of newness.
and the fear that all remains the same.

the kiss

the solitary kiss
so tenderly executed
belongs to others
as much as to ourselves.

its unveiling
drew others into an awareness.
and their disapproval
tainted its sweetness
and forbade its repetition.

even intimacy is never one's own
in a social world
that hungers for the exposure of others
while hiding its own indiscretions.

but the kiss lingers
in the endless repetition of the mind.
until it assumes a power of its own.
holding imagination in its firm grasp.

none can take this away.
or intrude and enter unbidden.
the secret of the heart remains
that longs to kiss again.

east vancouver night

like black sump oil
oozing from disused dodge
in tumbled-down shed
midnight darkness blankets all in east vancouver.

gnarled fingers from the abyss
pointing to this underworld
beckon the unsuspecting
to momentary intimacy
to seared flesh
psychedelic ecstacy.

dare to enter
into this darkest of nights.
this labyrinth of human pain.
don't come to stare.

resist turning on the lights.
leave your cheap charity behind.

come not with your ready-made answers
but stay and linger
long enough to know, to befriend
and own the darkness in your own life.

darkness ends in dawn.
the streets are empty.

the locals sleep their troubled sleep.
and you who came sleep in troubled solidarity.

in the sliver of light on this sombre morn
with the pain of the night that has gone before
a seed of hope was gradually born
that calls for the longest struggle.

this young man geoffrey

i must confess to little joy
in executing adam's ploy
to punish geoffrey in this way
when he should have the final say.

but if we must use words of rhyme
to get at geoffrey one more time
let's use them well
and weave a spell
without a plot
that says a lot
about this young man geoffrey.

but where to start
it is an art
just keeping pace
in the mad race
set by this young man geoffrey.

he must have slowed to father four
one hardly could have hoped for more
when he's gone all day
and i'd hate to say
he's up all night
when clients fight.

now it's not my task
to rip away the cloak and mask
and talk about the inner id
when geoffrey surely is full quid
there's heart and dreams
and so it seems
the will to care
to think and play and pray and share.

so who can tell what should be told
of energetic geoffrey forty year-old
he's far ahead of all the rest
so finally it does seem best
to continue on
in lilting song
to tell our young man geoffrey
that he's just great
and it's our blessed fate
to know this mate
who's set the pace
that leaves us out of the race.

for then he builds, repairs and mends
and studies all the latest trends
in therapy and social work
in helping others does not shirk
to do his bit
when does he sit
this active young man geoffrey?

well, he sits to eat
and it's some feat
to match our young geoffrey.
he dines at home to prepare
to go to dinner elsewhere.

but all these tales we know too well
and with the telling always swell
to enter realms of myth and fable
so that one is hardly able
to know the real man geoffrey.

your own life?

my own sweet child
made of a thousand tears and smiles
what hopes do you carry
that i have all but lost?

and what am i making of you
that i wish i was not?
and what are you discarding
to make the quest your own?
and what promises will you realise
that are yours and not mine?

broken community

the delicate fabric—
    of sharing life together
    joyful involvement
    hospitality and the welcome table
    trust and commitment as all are able;

    of communitarian hope
    economic prudence
    practical help and celebration
    in the hope of a new creation;

    of the vision of the acts community
    word, worship, koinonia and the common cup
    christ's presence that heals
    and fills us up;

lies tattered—
    torn by a thousand insecurities
    lost in a torrent of words

    marred by our frailties and fears
    washed in a torrent of tears.

    and in the giving we were violated
    in the sharing isolated
    in the caring we became lost
    bitter our food was the cost.

this tattered tapestry—
    now awaits in darkness
    the mystery of the cross
    the hope of resurrection
    the burning of our dross.

ode to a loved one

the face that laughed
with grey-blue eyes
and carefree brow
though wrinkled now
first fixed my gaze on you.

'twas strength and gentleness
bright though muted
that was your light
even undimmed now
that led me on
to see you won.

with swish of hair
and whispering tones
so many words were spoken
which wove their spell
a dialogue unbroken
revealing heart and soul.

and in our play
and groaning prayers
with music softly playing
we grew together
even more
than what our words were saying.

and side by side
through christ's clear call
we laboured in his garden
we learned of fruit and briers and thorns
and of the sinner pardoned.

and in the union of our love
first hesitant, uncertain
there came a seeking finding bond
where doubt was all transcended.

this love brought forth the gift of life.
your life sustained another.
and added to the daughters three
there came a little brother
and with the crown there came a cross
whose burden was no loss.

and in the times of dread and fear
with heavens baked like brass
and no voice from god was heard
but only the human whimper
you gave your woman love as gift
to stay the death of winter.

into the great silence

after all the words—
    aching
    caring
    vulnerable
    loving
wrenched from the wellsprings of our being,
let us again embrace the guileless silence.

not a silence of—
    emptiness
    questionless
    uncertainty
    unknowing.

but a silence that—
    shelters
    knows
    nurtures
    protects.

a night in greenwich village

electric sights
flashing, whirling
piercing night's darkness
with nocturn light.

shadows dance
on wall and street
with mechanical beat
of porter's feet.

instants of white
on ebony face
nodding on stoop
staring in space.

mind swims past
the grey and synthetic
the plaintive cry
of a guitar.

swirling journey
worlds afar
white mists feeling
colour and tar.

instants of white
on ebony face
hooded eyes
crashing in space.

shadows dance
electric sights
fading, dying
a new morn crying.

seeking journey

life is the long journey
away from the nurturing fountains
of the one who gently carried
our ever fragile frame.

torn from the source of life
we whimpering wend our way
soon cloak ourselves in self-suffiency
that masks our sheer dependency.

and in the places of fear and emptiness
we return to fondle breasts
long shrivelled in their aging
offering the comfort of impotence.

unfulfilled we wander elsewhere
living the taste of our brokenness
and resisting the bosom of the nubile
we continue the slow search for the womb of god.

the dreamer

like the starry-eyed boy who thought he—
    could fly like an eagle
    run like a cheetah
    turn asphalt into glittering gold
    hold the howling wind in his hand
    slay the dragon from the abyss,

so i thought i—
    could win your hidden heart
    soar with you on the up-winds of love
    enter your secret places
    find the sheltering oasis
    make you the final home-coming,

but boyhood dreams become the tinsel for nightmares
soaring dreams fall under a brutal sun
even the steady walker can falter on an even path
and love like a fallen glass in desert place makes no oasis.

i had so much wanted to hold this fragile dream
but like the brown edges of an old letter it crumbles
beneath fingers gnarled by aeons of waiting.

reflection

the unexpected came unbidden
breaking the steady grip of the familiar
leaving a smoke trail of uncertainty.

a whisper of an invitation was heard:
enter if you dare the spaces of reflection
don't close the door too quickly.

be still.
listen to inner murmurings.
discern.
embrace.

this confrontation with oneself is
troubling.
restless.
confusing.

one would gladly scurry to known paths
routines.
tradition.
rationalisations.
all the familiar signposts.

but it's too late.
the silver of light
the discerning thought

the new dream
has penetrated the straw façade that seemed like rock
and water gushes out.

the womb of god

like a flaming meteorite
she burst forth
propelled by those contraries
that fuse to make a mythic power
hang in azure space
whirling in the void
the icy crisp of nothingness
only to collide
and spin to where there is no edge.
here no lines are drawn
no barriers meet.

yet as silent as a sudden gasp
the power transforms
strangely fusing.
bearing all before
the fruit of god's own musing.

time

once upon a time…
the lilting stories of childhood
wrapped in dream-like mantle
that unravel with the loss of a virginal innocence.

in my time…
the repetitious reminders of the elderly
wrapped in layers of forgetfulness
that hold the past but have no future.

on time…
the mantra of our ordered world
driven by technique and efficiency
which longs for the art of transcendence.

about time…
the scathing voice of the other
rebuking the tardy and the slow
without grace and compassion.

timeless…
the seductive voice of the gods of industry
convincing us of what we need
that make us invincible.

in the fullness of time…
god sent his beloved son
as gift for all humanity
making eternity one.

Charles Ringma is regarded by many as a thinker, activist and contemplative. He has written in the areas of the social sciences and philosophy. He has worked as a missioner, researcher, and urban ministry practicioner, and has written numerous books on Christian spirituality. He has lived and worked in Europe, Australia, Asia and Canada, teaching theology and mission at Asian Theological Seminary, Manila and mission studies, philosophy and spirituality at Regent College, Vancouver. As a retired professor he continues to write and teach in various parts of the world.

Other Books by Charles Ringma

The Seeking Heart: A Journey with Henri Nouwen
Finding Naasicaa: Letters of Hope in an Age of Anxiety
Catch the Wind: A Precursor to the Emergent Church
*Life in Full Stride: Faith-Stretching Reflections for Christians in
    the Real World*
*Whispers from the Edge of Eternity: Reflections on Life and
    Faith in a Precarious World*

Cry Freedom with Voices From the Third World
Dare to Journey with Henri Nouwen
Let My People Go with Martin Luther King, Jr.
Resist the Powers with Jacques Ellul
Seek the Silences with Thomas Merton
Seize the Day with Dietrich Bonhoeffer
Wash the Feet of the World with Mother Teresa